An Amazing Secret
How to Benefit from …..

THE PLACEBO EFFECT

"If you can believe
All things are possible to him who believes"
Mark 9:23

Written by
Robert W. Wood D. Hp (Diploma in Hypnotherapy)

First published in U.K. 2019
By Rosewood Publishing

www.rosewood-gifts.co.uk

Robert W Wood D.Hp
Asserts the moral right to be identified
As the author of this work

Cover photograph by
Andrew Caveney BA (Hons)
www.andrewcaveneyphotography.co.uk

ISBN 978-0-9567913-5-1   BK16

How to Benefit from the Placebo Effect

Placebo, *an inactive substance administered to a patient who insists on receiving medication or who would benefit by the psychological deception*

This is a copy of Robert's script, the one that he has presented over many years at his Gemstone & Crystal Road shows.

It can be easily described as a cheerful, uplifting talk from the author of a series of 12 inspirational books collectively titled 'Power for Life'. A talk that helps to dispel myths, answers questions, and at the same time will reveal authentic, enlightening details about mind-boggling stuff. A fascinating inspirational talk intended to help to discover each and every ones hidden talent.

INTRODUCTION

Welcome, to set the scene I have written many books and given lots of talks on the History, the Science and the Mysteries that surround Gemstones and Crystals, but mainly the mysteries.

In Huddersfield, where I live, there is probably one of the largest wholesalers in Europe selling fossils, minerals and semi-precious gemstones. It trades as the Rock Shop in Ambleside, a shop found in the Lake District. Because I talk about the mysteries that surround gemstones and crystals I thought I ought to at least try and put my money were my mouth is and try to show you how to increase your chances for winning raffles, that's why you all have a free raffle ticket.

SOPHIES STORY

Let me give you an idea of what I mean by the mysteries: - so first, let me tell you the story about Sophie my 10 year old granddaughter. We were standing in front of a Tombola table at our local garden centre. This table was raising money for a local charity. Sophie noticed a lovely hand knitted kangaroo 'Skippy' and said out loud she would love to have it. Now with Tombola you have to draw out the lucky ticket, you can't just buy it. You have to win it. There were three ladies behind the table listening to Sophie saying she wanted it. Seeing a chance to get some money they encouraged her to have a go. Within the three ladies earshot I said to her, "I'll tell you a secret that might help you to win" and then we turned away from the table whilst I had a word with her, but out of the three ladies hearing. They all knew she wanted the kangaroo and on the first draw they couldn't believe it, and neither could I, she WON it.

You should have seen the amazement on those ladies faces and the absolute delight on Sophie's face. They didn't know what I had said to Sophie but later on I'll tell you.

ANN'S STORY (Sleep Well)

Another story, and there are many. Ann, a very good friend of mine, wittered and moaned that she couldn't sleep, in fact she witted and moaned that much I took pity on her and made her a very special bracelet, I called it 'Sleep Well'. I gave it to Ann, Ann then said "but what do I do with it? "Wear it" I said, a bit tongue in cheek, "it's been programmed".

I caught up with Ann a week or so later and I noticed that she was wearing her bracelet. She never said anything, so I asked her "why haven't you mentioned your bracelet Ann". Her reply was quite surprising, "I daren't" she said, "How do you mean 'you daren't? I asked. I don't want it to stop working, she said. What you are about to hear is an explanation; a certain way of thinking that may explain why for some people all this seems to work. Because of Ann's reaction it became the main reason why I came up with my range of 'themed' Power Bracelets.

One being 'To Loose A Stone' one of my best sellers and on occasions I have worn one to remind me to lose weight. I mentioned at one talk I seemed to lose one stone quite easily it was the second stone I struggle with. One lady suggested why not wear two, I'll have to try it. Another bracelet was 'To Remove Aches and Pains' very popular with a certain age group. Another got me into bother; it's called 'Fertility'. When the young lady, who had been trying to start a family for a while, she said it was down to me when she became pregnant and I had to explain what she actually meant. You get the idea.

MARCELLE VOGEL

I researched a gentleman called Marcelle Vogel, a scientist who worked for IBM the computer people. He travelled all around America demonstrating Crystal Healing. He created, mathematically, a twelve sided Quartz crystal pendulum and used it a bit like a body scanner. Believing that the body/mind communicated to the crystal revealing what was wrong with the patient/client. He did many things; one was he put the Crystal pendulum into water. The next part of this story will sound like it comes straight from 'Star Trek'.

He then produced a double terminated quartz crystal again mathematically cut with twelve sides believing that it somehow contained all the knowledge of the Universe. He could be right but how do you access it?

Let me suggest something to you, what if it's not the crystal but the belief in the crystal, I know it sounds like semantics but if it's the belief in the crystal then I think I can now empower you all with a knowledge that once you have grasped it's meaning, and you will, it could help you with the raffle at the end of my talk. Now I am not suggesting it's not the power in crystals, because many believe it is, only that there may be another way of explaining it. What if it's the belief? It's got to be worth exploring.

BIRTHSTONES / PARTY PLAN

Back to the beginning of my story; nearly thirty years ago I became involved with a company called – Burhouse. They paid me good money to research an idea of selling through party plan. I was brought in to create a script for a national sales force. We had a meeting and it was decided that the theme of the sales pitch could be based on birthstones, it was suggested that at least there would only be twelve instead of the thousands of gemstones and crystals that are out there.

That's how all this started and it was the birth of all my research, my books, and my Gemstone Crystal Road Shows. Incidentally the company happens to be a very strong Christian based company and didn't want to get involved with anything that might be a bit 'iffy' and so I started researching into twelve Birthstones.

At first I thought it would be very simple to find twelve birthstones, I thought you would just look it up in a book. So I read the likes of Mystic Meg, Patrick Walker, Russell Grant, Margery Orme and many many more. Only I found to my horror that they all seemed to be saying something different.

INSTUCTIONS
Now look inside your guide. *(it's reprinted on page 19)*

"Crystal Power"
Fact or Fiction

3

Now quite often people will say that I have got it wrong because they know there birthstone is a Diamond, a Ruby, a Sapphire, an Opal or Garnet etc. and you won't find any of these in my list. My list is softer, semi-precious rather than precious. Surprisingly in research I discovered that they didn't know how to cut a Diamond until the fifteenth century, apparently it takes a Diamond to cut a Diamond and Astrology, linked to birthstones is nearly six thousands year old.

MY LIST OF TWELVE BIRTHSTONES
So how did I get my list? Well, you may say I cheated; I had over seventeen different sources from all over the world. I had a headache for over three weeks but in the end I just took the mean average. So if for example the majority said Red Jasper was the birthstone for Aries then that was good enough for me and that's how I got my list, by using the 'mean average'.

So now I had a list of twelve birthstones, but did it mean anything? How could you test it? I am a bit of a cynic and so I came up with what I thought was a great idea. What if I passed a basket around containing all twelve birthstones in the shape of tumble stones to different groups and asked them to take out a stone that they liked and then I asked them what was there star sign.

I couldn't believe it, over 40% , even 50% and sometimes 60% seemed to pick out their own birthstones. However the biggest surprise was those who hadn't picked their own birthstone, many of them seemed to be picking out their opposite birthstones. So let me explain:-

CARL JUNG / MYERS BRIGGS
I think the only explanation that makes sense is that they were picking them out by colour, a colour they liked. For Example, I am Sagittarian which it's suggested that my birthstone would be a Sodalite, a bluey white stone from Russia. I can often be seen in a top jacket or shirt that's easily described as blue. My opposite star sign is Gemini, Black Onyx. You will often see me wearing black shoes, black trousers. I often wear my colours and I feel comfortable in them. So if you are a Sagittarian or a Gemini think of what colours you like.

Another example could be Aries. Red Jasper is suggested as an Aries birthstone. So if you are Aries do you like red and if not what do you think to Green, it's your opposite, Libra is suggested to be a Green Aventurine.

ASTROLOGY the SECRET CODE

It turns out that as we pass through 'mid-life' we flip over to our opposite star sign, it's called the 'Law of Polarity' that is the meaning of one is enhanced by the knowledge of the other. So whatever you have read now read your opposite star sign and blends the two together for a much fuller picture. If you do read your horoscope in the papers, read your opposite star sign as well for a fuller picture. *Page 20/21*

Where's all this coming from you may ask? Would you believe it started with a Swiss psychotherapist called Carl Jung? Even the Church uses it; astonishingly they have discovered that it's possible to separate the physical from the spiritual. In church it's called a Myers-Briggs typology and in my leaflet it's called 'Characteristics and Personalities' there is more in my book 'Astrology the Secret Code'

AN AMBIGUOUS LADY

When I started doing all this research, a friend of mine said, did I know that gemstones and crystals were mentioned in the Bible? "No I didn't know that so I asked" where? "I don't know where" he said, "I just know they are there.

Before I tell you what happened to me I want to show you a very famous picture of a women. This picture is no trick or an illusion it's just a picture of a women, the picture first appeared in Puck in 1915 so is now over one hundred years old.

Extra information

Before I show it to you I want to ask you what may sound like a daft question but bear with me. For those of you who can ride a bike can you remember the time when you couldn't and what was the difference.

I think the difference is 'knowing' you know you can do something. For example it took me three days to learn how to ride a bike. Do you know how I learnt? I fell off for three days but on the third day I stayed on and have stayed on ever since, something must have happened so let's call it for now 'a knowing'. Another example could be if you imagine a learner trying to drive a car and then look at them again a few months later, something as happened and I am calling this your 'Knowing'.

Another example could be swimming, it doesn't matter how long you have watched someone swim until you get into the water and take your feet off the floor, something happens.

What you are about to see will introduce you to your 'Knowing', the very thing that allows you to drive a car, ride a bike and swim and you will probably see your 'Knowing' within thirty seconds, the very thing that took me three days to learn. I promise you that although none of this may make sense just now, it will and it could help you to win raffles.

I know from experience that most people can see a young women in this picture, but some of you will be surprised to hear that, because some of you have quite a special gift, for you, you can only see an older women one who looks a little like a witch. If you see the old women and that's the picture that you saw first then hold up your hands I want to see were you are.

There aren't that many of you and I promise, you have quite a special gift. For the rest of you, if you see a young woman then look at her choker around her neck, that's the mouth of the older lady. The chin is the nose and the ear is the eye. Can any of you now say you have seen both pictures? I know not all of you will, but you will before the end of my talk.

WOMEN'S INSITUTE
I am going off script for a moment. I was giving a talk to a W.I. group many years ago and the Chairperson was the only one who could see the older women. The rest could only see the young women and that included her daughter.

However I must say I have never heard two women argue so much over a picture. The mother could only see the older women and the daughter the young one. They argued for over two minutes when there seemed to be a miracle. They both saw the other picture at the same time.

The silence was deafening and then the chairperson asked me what it meant, because she said she was the only one who could see the older women first. Well I said, a bit tongue in cheek "it means thank goodness you were there.

BACK TO THE BIBLE STORY

Remember I told you a friend had mentioned that he thought the gemstones and crystals that I was researching where in the bible. It was a Thursday morning when I managed to get hold of a bible, and the one I got had nearly 1400 pages in it, I know because I looked at the last page. I was thinking how you would find these stones in a Bible, short of having to read the whole thing. Now imagine this there are no P.C's at home and I hadn't heard of a 'concordance', that's a book that helps to find passages in the bible.

Something really strange seemed to happen. The book seemed to open up and I was drawn to an interesting story in Exodus. Moses was to bring the Israelites out of Egypt and Aaron who will become the first High Priest is asked by God to fashion a breast-piece and on this breast-piece he is to put on it twelve stones. These twelve stones will represent the twelve tribes of Israel. That's symbolism I thought, because in Astrology twelve stones represents the cycle of life, we call them birthstones.

Now within hours, on the same day, I found myself in the New Testament. (Rev. 21:19) Titled; The New Jerusalem. 'The city walls were decorated with every type of precious stones and the first foundation was Jasper, the Sixth Carnelian and the twelfth Amethyst. Now look at my list of Birthstones in your guide, the first is Aries – Red Jasper, the sixth is Virgo – Carnelian and finally the twelfth is Pisces – Amethyst. I have read the Gita the Hindu Bible and tried to study the Koran and I can tell you there are no other lists of twelve stones anywhere other than those two lists I have just given you.

Can you imagine how I felt when I realised what had just happened, passages don't just come out of books, and yet they did in my case.

PISCES THE FISH

Another thing that I had discovered in my research, that Pisces symbol is a fish.

Imagine crossing the two brackets over and you will get the shape of a fish. Have you ever seen a fish sign on the back of cars? I even have one on the back of my car and you can see I am wearing one.

The earliest Christians, who were being persecuted by the Romans, used a secret sign to show that they were followers of Christ, a sign of a fish. (IXOYE) 'Meaning, Jesus Christ Gods Son Saviour'. However, surprisingly I discovered in my research that Pisces was not only a unifying sign before it completes the cycle of life and goes back to Aries but was also a sign of a healer. What a lovely way of describing Jesus as a healer using this sign. Incidentally Astrology is over 6000 years old but Christianity only 2000 years old. So could this be the reason why they used a fish as a sign that they were followers of Christ? You won't hear this connection in Church unless I am giving the talk.

FISH FRYERS STORY

Many years ago I was giving a talk at a Methodist Church when afterwards one of the elders came up to me and said that his minister wore a fish like me and that he had told him a story. Apparently the minister had been to Blackpool, a northern seaside town, and for lunch he had had Fish and Chips, but it turned out to be the biggest fish he had ever seen, so he made a comment. The gentleman who had served him said "You know, we look after own, I noticed you are in the 'Fish Fryers' Association"

I was giving a talk some years later to a U3A social group when the Chairperson said that she owned a Fish and Chip shop and yes the Fish Fryers Association used the sign for their 'logo'. So you can use the sign if you are a Christian, A Pisces or have a chip shop, it's your choice.

NEGATIVE TRAITS

Back to my free guide; look at the negative traits, nobody seems to like them including me and I wrote this. I am a Sagittarian and I remember saying to my wife, "this is nothing like me" Robert, when you are in a mood, she said and so I didn't say anymore.

One night, at a talk, I overheard a woman reading out loud her daughter's husband's negative traits. She did it right she read straight across both star signs and blended them both together. They sounded terrible the way she said them and then she went on to say "do you know this has got him to a tee", I told her not to marry him I'm not surprised she's getting a divorce.

You will rarely see the negative traits in anyone unless they are ill or life is being particularly cruel. Think of what Bob Geldof had to go through to get Band Aid off the ground and you'll see that some of these traits can be quite useful. To give you an example you could carry a gun around with you and under certain circumstances it may give you confidence – but you don't have to shoot it. Remember, this information is coming from Carl Jung who was a student of Freud.

Before we move on to Crystal Healing let me explain just how powerful psychological profiling can be by giving you a very good example. Many years ago one of the largest Building Societies in the UK decided to go into direct banking. They advertised, and many from the banking sector applied including one young man who was surprised to get a call from them telling him his application hadn't succeeded however would he be interested in another position that they felt he had an aptitude for.

You could imagine he was a bit taken aback to say the least, on one hand they have said his application as failed and yet on the other they seem to be offering him the chance of an interview for another position. Curious he asked them what was the other position. They answered it was in their 'Debt Recovery Division' they said "we think you could be quite good at it". He is now one of the top men in that industry. So how did they know? It was because they had used psychological profiling on all the applicants. Be in no doubt, **Psychological Profiling** does work and when used properly it's a very powerful tool. As I have mentioned in the Church it's known as a Myers-Briggs Typology and I have taken poetic licence to reproduce some of it here, but you must be the judge of all this yourselves.

PART 2 - HOLISTIC HEALING

VIBRATIONAL FREQUENCIES

Let's now change the subject, we are moving away from Birthstones, lucky talismans onto Holistic Healing, Holistic meaning the whole thing. That is; taking into account somebodies physical, mental and social conditions in the treatment of their illness. According to the Holistic Healers they seem to suggest that Gemstones and Crystals have vibrational frequencies, and they do, and by coming close to a particular crystal it can help to bring one back into balance, back to health. I suppose it's a little like swimming with dolphins. They have the reputation for healing especially for those that feel this could be of benefit to them. Crystal Healing has the same reputation.

As a Christian I am not suggesting any one should worship stones, the way I would put it is, you wouldn't dream of worshiping aspirin just because it may help with headaches but years ago they didn't have chemists and this is what they used, it's as simple as that.

MENU ON THE BACK PAGE OF MY FREE GUIDE *Page 22*

If you want to follow me, go to the back page on my guide, were you will see all the same stones, in the same running order but on a different subject, healing. I'll skirt round it, but this will give you an idea. They say Red Jasper is good for emotional problems; Black Onyx can instil calm and serenity, Tiger Eye, a confidence stone, Green Aventurine acts as a general tonic and Rhodonite is said to improve your memory, Obsidian Snowflake your eye sight, if you wanted to become pregnant get a Moonstone. It may have helped my daughter. She got married in the Dominican Republic many years ago. I gave her a lovely Moonstone pendant from India; because it's not only a fertility stone but a good luck stone. It must have worked she had only been married for just over a year when we had our first granddaughter and a year or so later a second granddaughter. A couple of years later we had another granddaughter, this meant I had to swop our car; some of you will probably know you can't get three booster seats side by side in most cars. A year or so later we had a grandson. I suggested she gave the Moonstone back but she said she couldn't, why I asked, because apparently she loaned it out. That moonstone has got some history.

ROSE QUARTZ

If somebody had asked me which gemstone was the most popular healing crystal I would have to say Rose Quartz? It came up time after time, again and again in research. You will read on the back of my guide that it says when coupled with Hematite can work wonders on Aches and Pains, any one with aches and pains that would like to work wonders on? We may be coming to an interesting bit.

At this point in my talks I would show a piece of Rose Quartz saying it probably came from Spain and then a piece of Hematite that probably only came from Cumbria in the UK.

I was giving a talk at Pinderfields Hospital in Yorkshire England many years ago when a gentleman in the audience asked me if I knew that hematite was an iron ore. "Yes" I said, I have even been down a hematite mine. Then he said but did you know that when placed near a quartz crystal it will excite its energy. No I didn't know that, do you mean what I have been saying all these years could be true? Yes he said.

EARTH SCIENCE

At this stage I would show a beautiful piece of Rock Crystal.

Let me change the subject for a moment into earth science. This is a lovely piece of clear Rock Crystal that's often found growing inside rocks. If you analysed it, in its simplest form then it's just silicon and oxygen. Earth's crust is made up of similar. We even have a little liquid silicon within our bodies. Now if in nature this was anywhere near iron it would change colour to purple – Amethyst. Magnesium and Titanium it would be Rose Quartz. I have now linked Clear Rock Crystal and Rose Quartz. Have you heard of Quartz watches? You must know how accurate they are.

When my father bought me my first wrist watch, it said on the back plus or minus. What that meant was if the watch was going too fast I could slow it down and if it was going too slow I could speed it up. Mine ran on tea-cakes and then I heard some adverts on this new programme in the UK called ITV, watches that only lost a second or two a year. A second or two a year! I couldn't believe it, my watch would lose a second or two a minute.

What science discovered within my lifetime was that if you send an electrical charge through a quartz crystal it vibrates at a frequency of 32,768 times per second. Imagine the vast size of that number per second. In a watch the crystal requires very little power, power that is often supplied by a very tiny battery.

Now for the technical bit.
As the atoms in the quartz vibrate they emit very precise electronic pulses. These pulses are then channelled through microchip circuity, where they are successively halved in a series of 15 steps. The result is really astounding: it produces a single, constant pulse per second and that one single pulse is precisely one second and I mean precisely. Now science can now reproduce quartz in laboratories and amazingly it still maintains the same frequency.

Did you know that the space shuttle had windows and it isn't 'Pilkington Glass?' In the space shuttle the windows are three feet thick and lined in gold and it's made from 'fused quartz. Its quartz melted down and reformed.
I show a fused Quartz obelisk at this point.
Then I go on to say;
I could hold this in my hand and put a blow torch on it and you would see it glow but it wouldn't transmit the heat. For health and safety reasons jewellers can no longer use asbestos mats, so what do they use? They use fused quartz mats, the heat shield on the space shuttle is made with fused quartz. Halogen lamps are so hot that they are encased with fused quartz. Quartz crystal is just amazing.

You would have heard that at the heart of all computers there are microchips and what are microchips but a piece of quartz. I told you that quartz is just silicon and oxygen well that's why they call the heart of all microchip production in California, 'Silicon Valley'. There was a time when pure quartz was more valuable than gold, at least until they discovered how to reproduce it in laboratories.

Here's a school boy trick, take any two pieces of quartz and rub them firmly together and you'll see them light up, it's quite spectacular. Another way of showing you this is with an oven gas lighter available from any supermarket.

Now for a bit more technical stuff
It's called a 'piezoelectric' effect, from the Greek word 'piezo' meaning 'I press' If you have a gas oven you may have used a special lighter-wand to create a spark. This special tool has a piece of quartz built into it, which releases energy (the spark) when it is used, and it works without the need of a battery. While natural quartz is abundant, it is rarely perfect, with all its 'rogue' trace elements rendering it unsuitable for commercial use. So piezoelectric crystals are now produced synthetically in the laboratory. Although synthetic, they still have the same atomic structure and properties as their natural counterparts.

ELIXIR OF LIFE
Leaving earth science behind lets go back to our guide and the back page. Look at number nine, Sodalite, it says when coupled with Rhodonite can produce the 'elixir of life'. Sounds great, I looked it up in a dictionary, it said it was rejuvenating, and produces youthfulness. It's at this stage I put the two stones into a glass of water and drink it. I remember being invited to speak to a group that I had been to some years earlier. Although she may have me confused with someone else she said when we met again, "you are looking younger Robert" and so just in case I take another drink.

PART 3

DO I BELIEVE IN ALL THIS?
People often will ask me "do you believe in all this"? Maybe one of the reasons why a company paid me good money could be my background. I have always been involved in sales and marketing. I looked into many different religions before I became confirmed into the Church of England. I had studied philosophy, when I have the time I meditate. If prayer is asking then meditating is listening for the answers and they seem to come. I am also a qualified Hypnotherapist, not in private practice, I couldn't afford the insurance. You only have to have a client trip up when leaving your office and you could get a law suit.

These days everybody seems to be suing everybody else. Good news if you're a lawyer. As a Hypnotherapist you won't be surprised if I tell you that I think maybe all this could be in the mind and not the stones. Don't get me wrong it could be the stones, but I think we could be on stronger ground if we say if it's all in the mind.

THE SECRET FORMULA REVEALED

Let me now empower you all with knowledge, that once you have grasped it's meaning, and I know you will, it could help you with my raffle at the end and any other raffles.

Before I tell you of a secret formula that I discovered I am going to give you all an anchor so at least you will know what it is that I am talking about. Have you heard of the Placebo Effect? In case you haven't it's whenever they test new drugs. How the trials work is that they give the proper drug to half of the patients and the other half just a sugar coated pill, a pretend. However, and this is the heart of where we are going, for those who believed that they had been given the proper medicine, but hadn't some, not all, are cured, it must be the most natural form of healing known to man, although it's based on a lie, there no side effects. *What would you do if you knew how all this worked?*

Just before I share this formula with you, let's explore this idea of belief. In Mark 9:23 in the New King James Version Bible, Jesus said to him, "if you can believe all things are possible to him who believes" "Help me to believe".

I could talk about Quantum physics and Molecular structures but most would be bored silly. So I will let a 14 year old girl explain just how all this could work; she explains it much better than I can.

With a face like thunder she came home from school one day shouting "I've no chance, he's the most popular boy in the year, will he look at me! Will 'e-heck. My clothes don't fit, I am over weight and I have spots. She certainly had verbal diarrhoea. When the young lady calmed down it was suggested to her that there may be a formula that just might help her. Did she know that when imagination and willpower are in conflict, imagination will always win its set in granite and then she was told how to use it?

Two or three weeks later she came home from school with her face brimming "he's asked me out" she shouted "and all the girls want to know what she had been told. I bet they did. Except Celia, Celia's going round school telling everybody that her mentor, me, must be a witch. Who's Celia? Her farther is a Minister in the local Church. Was I in bother, but before I tell you what I had told her and what I had told my Granddaughter with the Skippy story, there is another true story that links in rather nicely.

HOW TO WIN

Both I and my wife have regularly gone to Spain by Coach (incidentally we fly now) and the couriers to raise money always sold raffle tickets, this is why I always finish with a free raffle. The year I was doing all my research, whilst going on holiday, I had said to my wife, a bit 'tongue in cheek' I'll show you the magic, I'll show you how to win. We were upstairs on a double decker coach going through France, when it came over on the 'Tannoy' that the first prize was a magnum of champagne and the second prize was two bottles of wine. I turned to my wife and said I didn't fancy the champagne but I did fancy the wine, what did she think? I think you are crackers, she said, you need a holiday, it's got to you all this research, but I was going on holiday. Now would you believe it, I did win the two bottles of wine. I didn't let on but I was just as surprised as she was.

BINGO STORY

Two weeks later when we were coming back home on a different coach and with different couriers this time instead of a raffle they decided to play bingo. I must admit I find bingo quite stressful. However I bought a card and said almost jokingly to my wife, I'll show you again how all this works, I'll show you the magic, I'll show you how to win. "I don't know how you did it last time" she said, "but you have no chance", there must have been more than 50 people playing. "You watch" I said quite angrily. What happened next nearly scared me to death. The numbers just seemed to come out almost one after the other until I only needed just one number for a full house, number 14 and then she called it. I had watched this and so had my wife. The courier came upstairs and checked my card, and yes I had won, but what had I won? it turned out to be twenty four tins of larger. They are in the cubbyhole downstairs she said pick them up on you way out.

I nearly got an hernia trying to carry twenty four tins of larger and two suitcases. So what are the chances of winning both times when I had said in advance that I would, is it all just a coincidence or is there something else that may be at play?

AN EXPLANATION
Let me tell you what I had told the young lady. I would have loved to have told her why didn't she pray? But if I had said that I probably wouldn't have seen her again. However, I did, she just didn't realise it at the time that I had, a bit of subterfuge, I was using the 'placebo effect'.

I suggested to her that she drew a heart on a piece of paper and put her initials and his on to it and then she should fold it up and wear it as close to her heart as she could.

As often as she could I wanted her to take it out of her pocket, open it up and do something she had said was impossible. Could she imagine him, with feeling, him asking her out? Not the other way round that would be cheating? "Yes of course I can" she said "I'm always doing that" well how would you feel if he did ask you out? "Marvellous" she said, well there you are that's the key, now turn it.

Three or four weeks later he did ask her out and they went out for about four weeks, and then do you know what happened next? She ditched him.

Now with my wife on the coach it's the same formula but a different way of doing it. You see I could clearly hear her in my imagination saying "that's typical Robert you have won again". Believe me I don't win that often, I only wished that I did, but what I did was to imagine how I would *feel* if I did win. With my granddaughter I asked her to pretend she had won and how did she feel? Imaging a feeling is not as easy as it may sound, but it's what I did. Wow! Some people have said that I have been talking about a positive mental attitude and in a way they are right, but it was not where I was coming from. In the Bible there are just two lines were Jesus said, and I believe him.

Mark 11:22 therefore I tell you, whatever you ask for in prayer, believe that you have received it and it will be yours. So how do you believe, well that's easy, but this is the secret, this is the code, you must add a feeling an emotion. There is a coded language out there and when you know this code this is dead easy. Whenever I hear someone say to me, and I hear it often *'That's Strange'* or *'You Won't Believe* **This'** or *'I Was Thinking of You'* or *'That's A Coincidence'* I always listen to what comes next because that is the power at work.

JESUS PICTURE
An example of a coincidence. I was walking through town on a Friday afternoon when I had a brainstorm, if only I could find that picture. I went into a specialised gift shop and described a picture I would like to find, a very unusual picture and to my relief they knew what it was I was talking about. Then the bomb shell "I know what you mean but I haven't a clue where you could find it". Saturday came and then Sunday, I was still feeling disappointed but by Monday, if I am honest I had forgotten about it, Monday had come with its own problems. At Monday teatime my daughter came in from work, she said her friend Penny had been to a car boot sale on Sunday and had bought a very unusual tapestry. She said have a look I have tried to draw you a picture. Well I looked and then did I look, it was the picture I had gone into a specialised gift shop three days earlier and asked for. I promise you nobody had known I had called into that shop, let alone what I had asked for. If that's not a *'coincidence'* I don't know what is.

HOW TO ACTIVATE THE HIDDEN POWER BK7
This is the book that you have been listening to, see the picture of the young/old women in the back and now look what's on the first page JESUS

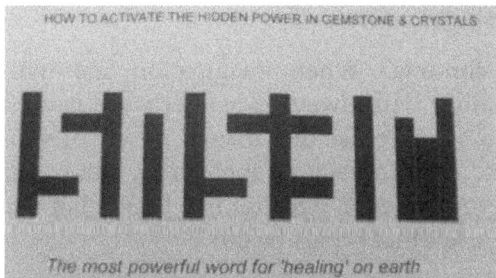

HOW TO ACTIVATE THE HIDDEN POWER IN GEMSTONE & CRYSTALS

The most powerful word for 'healing' on earth

Just to give you a clue it's upside down.

I had gone into a Christian book shop and asked for a picture of Jesus, one that you can't see. Hang on that sounds daft so let me explain, I had been in a retreat and on the wall was a plaque, when I first saw it, it just looked like Chinese lettering, it didn't make sense. Next time I looked at it, it now said a word, it probably said Jesus is Lord; after all I was in a religious retreat. The guy in the shop said, "I know what you mean" great where can I get one? I haven't a clue he said, I know what you mean but I don't know where you would get one. Three days later my daughter walk in with the very same picture I had walked in a shop three days earlier and asked for.

Another way of showing you this power, the power we are talking about. Look at the picture on the front of your guide. Imagine you are in the picture, can you walk up those steps or are you underneath.

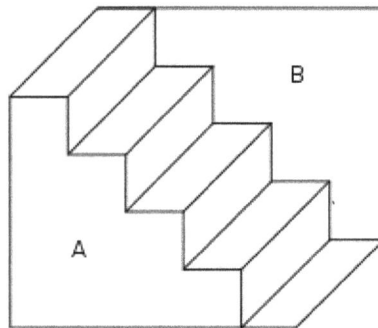

Look for just a few seconds and you will see the picture change. If you feel you in the picture you can walk up the steps then wait a few seconds and it will change, you will feel you are underneath. Let me explain what is happening, its universal law there are in fact two ways of seeing this picture and you sub-conscious, your 'knowing as got to show you the second picture.

Remember the formula? When imagination and will power are in conflict, imagination will always win. Let's try it out, let's draw the raffle. When you begin to use the 'magic' power of your subconscious, then you'll notice small miracles happening around you, and more will come. What do you believe? Because maybe it's not the thing believed in, but the belief itself that brings results.

The law of life is the law of belief, and belief could be summed up briefly as a thought in the mind.

Welcome to the world of
Rosewood gifts and Publishing

If you like natural products, hand-crafted gifts including Gemstone Jewellery
Objects of natural beauty – the finest examples from Mother Nature,
Tinged with an air of Mystery – then we will not disappoint you..

We have on display:-
Special gifts with Attitude,
Gifts inspired to lift the spirits
Gifts that capture the imagination.
Gifts will be available to purchase after the presentation.

Today's talk and display is presented by:-
Robert W. Wood D.Hp
(Diploma in Hypnotherapy)

" *Crystal Power* "
Fact or Fiction
Based on the science & mysteries surrounding Gemstones & Crystals.

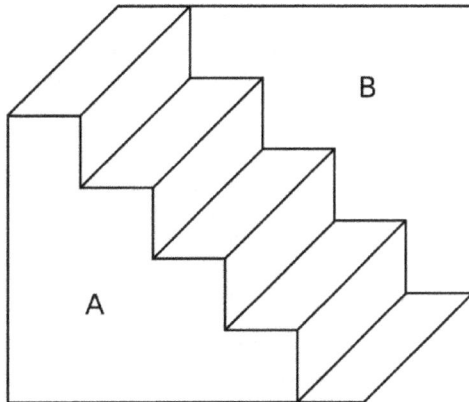

You can discover your "knowing" with the help of this picture.

www.rosewood-gifts.co.uk
email:- **info@rosewood-gifts.co.uk**

Robert is the Author of 'Power for Life' and 'An Alternative view on Crystal Healing'
Both books are now available from Amazon Kindle and in paperback from 'Create
Space'

Characteristics and Personalities

ARIES   Dates: 21st March – 20th April   Birthstone **RED JASPER**
The Ram Arians have a straightforward and positive attitude to life. They need adventure and like to take risks. They are passionate and sexy people but can be aggressive and dominating.

Positive Traits   Courageous, enthusiastic, independent, forthright, active energetic.
Negative Traits   Extravagant, impulsive, brash, selfish, impatient, headstrong.

TAURUS   Dates: 21st April – 21st May   Birthstone **ROSE QUARTZ**
The Bull   Taureans are very loyal, sensible and reliable but need securityand routine in their lives. They are passionate lovers but can be very possessive and stubborn.

Positive Traits   Sincere, reliable, faithful, solid and dependable.
Negative Traits   Obsessive, intransigent, possessive, naïve, obstinate, plodding.

GEMINI   Dates: 22nd May – 21st June   Birthstone **BLACK ONYX**
The Twins   Very chatty, lively people who make good salespeople with a natural ability to sell. Gemini's can be charming, flirty and fun, but can be impatient to others.

Positive Traits   Humorous, communicative, ingenious, witty, versatile, spontaneous.
Negative Traits   Emotionally detached, inclined to exaggerate, flighty, restless, fickle.

CANCER   Dates: 22nd June – 22nd July Birthstone **MOTHER OF PEARL**
The Crab   Cancerians are very nice, caring and sensitive, with a tendency to worry. They can be moody but are very faithful and supportive to partners making very good long-term friends.

Positive Traits   Industrious, thrifty, loyal, sympathetic, sensitive and tenacious.
Negative Traits   Secretive, capricious, cloying, over-emotional, touchy, clinging.

LEO   Dates: 23rd July – 23rd August   Birthstone **TIGER EYE**
The Lion   Leos are leaders and organisers who love life. They are generous and like to spend money. They are dominating and very vain but can be warm and enthusiastic.

Positive Traits   Benevolent, hospitable, forgiving, affectionate, regal, magnanimous.
Negative Traits   Self-centred, uncompromising, vain, gullible, domineering.

VIRGO   Dates: 24th August – 22nd September   Birthstone **CARNELIAN**
The Virgin   Virgos are workers, practical and neat in every way. They can be perfectionists and critical of others. They are also very genuine people who tend to worry.

Positive Traits   Painstaking, analytical, studious, considerate, discriminating.
Negative Traits   Self-effacing, prone to worry, detached, sceptical, cynical.

Plus My Suggested Birthstones

LIBRA
The Scales
Dates: 23rd Sept. – 23rd Oct   Birthstone GREEN AVENTURINE
This is the sign of fair play and harmony. Librans are charmers who enjoy socialising and do not like to feel left out. They manage to appear calm in situations but can be indecisive.

Positive Traits   Gracious, cheerful, charming, refined, diplomatic, impartial.
Negative traits   Manipulative, procrastinating, indecisive, impressionable.

SCORPIO
The Scorpion
Dates: 24th Oct – 22nd November   Birthstone RHODONITE
Scorpios are energetic, intense, sensual people. They are secretive and jealous with a tendency to be over-possessive with partners, but enjoy an active sexual relationship.

Positive Traits   Resourceful, decisive, penetrating, persuasive, competitive focused.
Negative Traits   Resentful, vindictive, sarcastic, jealous, suspicious, cunning.

SAGITTARIUS
The Centaur
Dates: 23rd November – 21st December   Birthstone SODALITE
These are hunters who need freedom and stimulation. Sagittarians are enthusiastic and fun-loving, with a thirst for knowledge. They need a lot of understanding, especially within relationships.

Positive Traits   Frank, logical, kind, generous, optimistic, honest.
Negative Traits   Extravagant, quarrelsome, blunt, dictatorial, irresponsible.

CAPRICORN
The Goat
Dates: 22nd Dec – 20th Jan   Birthstone OBSIDIAN SNOWFLAKE
Capricorns are ambitious, hardworking, independent, individuals who enjoy good taste. They have a tendency to be bossy and stubborn, with a need for security and stability.

Positive Traits   Profound, patient, practical, efficient, ambitious, hard-working.
Negative Traits   Gloomy, snobbish, materialistic, arrogant, intolerant, pessimistic.

AQUARIUS
The Water Carrier
Dates: 21st January – 19th February   Birthstone BLUE ONYX
Aquarians make excellent friends as they are understanding and faithful. They are complex characters, original and magnetic. They can appear eccentric at times and have very lively traits.

Positive traits   Humane, trustworthy, caring, intuitive, friendly, broad-minded.
Negative Traits   Unpredictable, moody, rebellious, stubborn, abrupt, impersonal.

PISCES
The Fish
Dates: 20th February – 20th March   Birthstone AMETHYST
Pisceans are creative and imaginative but sometimes lack confidence. They are very caring, sensitive, kind characters. Lack of ambition is one of their negative traits, together with vagueness and indecision.

Positive Traits   Unassuming, courteous, artistic, imaginative, gentle, lenient.
Negative Traits   Apologetic, irrational, changeable, self-pitying, hypersensitive.

The above are extracts from my book 'Astrology the Secret Code'
Discover the "The Law of Polarity" the meaning of one is enhanced
by the knowledge of the other.

PLEASE NOTE:- The following information is not authoritative, but a fluid interpretation from many sources. Any information given in this guide is not intended to be taken as a replacement for medical advice. Any person with a condition requiring medical attention should consult a qualified doctor or therapist.

THE SUGGESTED HEALING POWERS OF CRYSTALS

1. RED JASPER can help those suffering from emotional problems by balancing the physical & emotional needs. A powerful healing stone that's invigorating.
Good for:- Kidney, Bladder. Said to be able to improve the sense of smell.

2. ROSE QUARTZ can help with migraine and headaches. Coupled with Hematite, can work wonders on aches and pains throughout the whole body.
Good for:- Spleen, kidneys and circulatory system. A well liked powerful healer.

3. BLACK ONYX instils calm and serenity; diminishes depression. A protective stone worn in times of conflict, a student's friend as it encourages concentration.
Good for:- Bone marrow and the relief of stress. Protects against unwise decisions.

4. MOTHER OF PEARL calms the nerves, aptly dubbed the 'sea of tranquillity', it creates physical harmony of a gentle but persuasive kind. Indicates treasure.
Good for:- Calcified joints and the digestive system, relaxes and sooths.

5. TIGER EYE 'the confidence stone' inspires brave but sensible behaviour with great insight and clearer perception. Fights hypochondria and psychosomatic diseases.
Good for :- Bladder, kidneys and liver, a stone that invigorates and energises.

6. CARNELIAN a very highly evolved healer. Brings joy, sociability and warmth. A good balancer; can help you to connect with your inner self. The 'friendly' one.
Good for:- Rheumatism, arthritis, depression, neuralgia; good for concentration.

7. GREEN AVENTURINE acts as a general tonic on a physical level. If left in water overnight, it can be used to bathe the eyes and similarly to treat skin irritations.
Good for:- For relieving anxiety and fears. A good luck stone, a lucky talisman.

8. RHODONITE improves memory, calms the mind and reduces stress. Gives confidence and self-esteem. Cheers the depressed, preserves youth and retards ageing.
Good for:- Emotional trauma, mental breakdown, spleen, kidneys and heart.

9. SODALITE imparts youth and freshness to its wearer. Calms and clears the mind, enhancing communication and insight with the higher self. Brings joy and happiness.
Good for:- When coupled with Rhodonite it produces the 'Elixir of Life'.

10. OBSIDIAN SNOWFLAKE a powerful healer, brings insight and understanding. Keeps energy well grounded, clears subconscious blocks. A very lucky talisman.
Good for:- Eyesight, stomach and intestines, alleviates viral and bacterial infections.

11. BLUE ONYX a super charger of energy. It can give a sense of courage and helps to discover truth. Instils calm and serenity; diminishes depression, gives self-control.
Good for:- Stress, ear infections and often found in rosaries; it helps with devotion.

12.AMETHYST Bishop's stone, stone of healing, of peace, of love. St. Valentine implied it was one of the best gifts between lovers. Aids creative thinking, relieves insomnia.
Good for:- Blood pressure, fits, grief and insomnia. Aids creative thinking.

13 HEMATITE a very optimistic inspirer of courage and magnetism. It lifts gloominess and depression and when used in conjunction with Carnelian, can prevent fatigue.
Good for:- Blood, spleen and generally strengthens the body, helps with stress.

14. ROCK CRYSTAL enlarges the 'aura' of everything near to it, and acts as a catalyst to increase the healing powers of other minerals. It holds a key role in all holistic practices. *Good for:-* The mind and soul, strengthening, cleansing and protecting.

15 MOONSTONE thought to act as a lucky talisman when given by the groom to his bride. Claimed, in India, to promote long life and happiness. It soothes away stress and anxiety. *Good for:-* Period pains and other kindred disorders. A powerful fertility stone.

NOTES

See my web site for all the details on my books and various gifts.

www.rosewood-gifts.co.uk

"Power for Life-Power Bracelets"

Especially for those who can enjoy that feeling of connecting with the esoteric nature of Gemstones& Crystals, these gifts are ideal for you.

Power Bracelets have evolved over many years and have gained a lot of inspiration from the power beads worn by, for an example, the Dalai Lama; and also the rosary beads used for devotion in many churches including the Catholic Church. Buddhist would know them more by the name 'Mala' (ma-la) from an ancient Sanskrit language roughly meaning when translated "Rose or Garland".

Luck:-
Although there's no basis in science for luck and maybe luck is only an illusion of control, but control is what we try to seek in a random world. Themed 'Power Gems' can give the owner a sense of preparedness, a feeling of control and encourage a more positive outlook on life, which in itself may give us that 'edge', an extra push to help improve our life, and change it for the better.

Our journey through life is all about personal empowerment and the freedom of choice, and what we can do with it. Be prepared, with help of our Themed 'Power Gems' don't be surprised when positive changes start to come.

Extract from my book, Lucky Gemstone and Crystal Talismans, Charm and Amulets by Robert W Wood D.Hp

An Amazing Secret
How to Benefit from ....
THE PLACEBO EFFECT

Over many years this has become an electrifying script; the one that Robert as presented whilst delivering his many Gemstone and Crystal 'Road Shows'

"Offering the potentiality beyond your wildest dreams
For Health, Wealth and Happiness"

This book is for everyone who is inspired to seek information, knowledge and empowerment. Sometimes the truth is so evident and yet so many seem to miss it. By expanding your consciousness, it will help to set you free.

By rethinking about life and God you can easily start and change your future. Be astonished at just how powerful you really are. We all have a natural built in help system. Some know it as the 'Placebo Effect' and it seems to be able to explain the healing powers of gemstones and Crystals. Begin a new spiritual journey now and awaken your mind to the truth and discover a belief that can set you free.

"When imagination and willpower are in conflict,
Imagination will always win.
It's set in granite."
"and I'll tell you how to use it"
Robert W Wood D.Hp

Rosewood Publishing
www.rosewood-gifts.co.uk

ISBN 978-0-9567913-5-1

£3.95

www.rosewood-gifts.co.uk

REF: BK16

www.ingramcontent.com/pod-product-compliance
Lightning Source LLC
Chambersburg PA
CBHW060549030426
42337CB00021B/4504